Kickstart Your Novel

Kickstart Your Novel

A toolkit for aspiring writers

Julie Proudfoot

Powerful Owl Press

CONTENTS

	DEDICATION	vii
	Dear Writer	1
1	Finding Your Idea	2
2	Exploring Your Idea	4
3	Discovering Your Characters	7
4	Creating An Outline	10
5	Outline Template A	21
6	Outline Template B	22
7	Filling In Your Outline	23
8	Moving Forward	28
9	Final Tips And Tricks	30
	ABOUT THE AUTHOR	36
	NOTES	37
	NOTES	39

Copyright © 2022 by Julie Proudfoot

All rights reserved. No part of this book may be reproduced in any manner whatsoever without written permission except in the case of brief quotations embodied in critical articles and reviews.

First Printing, 2022

(To the cat,
and also, to the dog.)

Dear Writer

Dear writer,

Welcome to *Kickstart Your Novel*. As an author and teacher of writing, I know the desire and passion to write is sometimes not enough to get a novel written; the road from idea to manuscript can be confusing and daunting. *Kickstart Your Novel* is a grassroots, simple-to-access, concise guide to the tools I find the most useful for getting first drafts on the page.

Every writer has their own set of tips and tricks that work for them, and I encourage you to take from here what's most useful for you and your writing habits, and then come back to the rest if and when you need to. Whether you're writing for therapy, to get published or just for fun, my mission is to help you lay the foundations of your work, so that you can then progress to the next phase of rewriting, editing and polishing your novel.

The important thing is to get your words on the page—then you've got something to work with. The expression 'you can't edit a blank page' is where we begin.

Julie Proudfoot

1

Finding Your Idea

To begin any piece of writing, you need an idea. Inspiration for ideas can be found in many places:

- News and current affairs
- Moments or events from your life that you can embellish
- Your own interests and passions

Your idea should call to you and grab your attention; remember, you'll be sharing the ride with it for some time, so you need to enjoy the process of getting to know it inside and out.

News and current affairs

News sites on the internet provide unlimited stories and scenarios. Search your favourite news platform or follow them on social media. Keep a notebook handy and log stories that grab your attention. Old magazines in waiting rooms are an excellent source of ideas, and using them for research is a great way to fill that time.

Past moment/event

Moments in time from my own life are one of my favourite sources of story ideas. One example is an hour or so that I spent inside a caravan with a family member. This was my father's caravan; he had recently passed away in a car accident, and one of my family members and I were cleaning the van in preparation to sell it. We were stuck inside for some time, as other family members were busy scrubbing and pressure washing the outside of the van. Inside, we had meaningful conversations while my father's empty slippers sat nearby. I knew this would be a wonderful moment in time that I could transform into a story featuring plenty of insightful conversation, confessions and tender moments.

Interests and passions

Interests and passions that are important to you will provide endless stories to write about. Are you interested in sports? Health? Faith? Gardening? Aliens? Genealogy? Search for these keywords on the internet to read what people are reporting and commenting about your passions.

2

Exploring Your Idea

Once an idea has found its way to you, it's time to examine it more closely and draw out the elements that you'll need to begin outlining your story.

One of the most important elements in story writing is conflict or a struggle, either emotionally or physically. This is needed to drive your story forward, and the overcoming of this conflict/struggle will be the resolution of your story. You might choose to incorporate multiple conflicts into your story, but for simplicity, we'll work on the idea of just one.

For example, your character might struggle or conflict with another person; inner demons; a company, government or other large corporation; a natural phenomenon, such as a tornado or wild beast; a science-fiction-oriented element, such as aliens or the universe; or fantasy elements, such as a wizard, elves or dragons.

To help draw out the conflict within an idea, I like to begin with the concept that an engaging story proposes a question, and then, over the course of the narrative, answers that question.

To create your question, you'll need to drill down into your idea. I like to use a three-pronged tool I call the **What if ... and ... but ...**

scenario. This is a linear way of telling a story, where events occur one after the other in time. (Once you finish your first draft, you might choose to shuffle your chapters and paragraphs around—much like the blocks in a game of *Tetris*—for more impact or intrigue, or to hold back information from your reader until later. You can have fun with this in the rewriting and editing phases, but for the purpose of creating your first draft, it's easier to adhere to a linear timeline.)

To help you create your question, here are some examples of the **What if ... and ... but ...** scenario to show you how it works.

Example: News / current affairs idea

On an alternative news site, I found a story about a car buried in the centre of the Moon:

What if ... a 1950s car is thought to be embedded in the centre of the Moon, **and ...** an expedition to retrieve the car sets out, **but ...** the expedition party becomes trapped inside the centre of the Moon?

Example: Moment-in-time idea

What if ... two siblings are stuck inside a caravan for many hours **and ...** find themselves discussing past family incidents, **but ...** their perspectives are conflicting, and this causes tension.

Example: From my first novel

The **What if ... and ... but ...** scenario in my first novel, *The Neighbour*, looks like this:

What if ... a man accidentally causes the death of a neighbour's child, **and ...** holds the secret that this child was actually his, **but ...** the emotional pain and secrecy undo him?

Example: From my current work-in-progress novel

The **What if ... and ... but ...** scenario in the manuscript I'm currently working on (at time of writing) looks like this:

What if ... artificially intelligent robots are used in the health industry, **and ...** a person utilises a sex bot to treat erectile disfunction, **but ...** their relationship with the robot influences the way they treat people in their life?

These four little words—**What if ... and ... but ...**—will become significant markers in your story outline. They'll give you a clear sense of what you're writing: you'll know what kicks your story off (**What if ...**), where your story is going (**and ...**) and how your character will be tested (**but ...**).

This will be the bones of your story, and it will be your guiding star to look to if you become stifled by the largeness of your story or lose sight of your goals. You may also find that, as your story evolves and you begin to know your characters, you come back to your **What if ... and ... but ...** to tweak it here and there.

3

Discovering Your Characters

To help you get a clear sense of who you're going to be 'inhabiting' as you write, it's a good idea to make notes about your main character. You might have created more than one protagonist in your story, but for this purpose, we'll work with the idea of one main character.

You don't need to have all the information about your character clear in your mind before you begin to write, but having a solid understanding is going to be helpful. As you work through your story, your character will likely change and develop before your eyes; this is a normal process, and you won't fully get to know a character until you start writing about them or writing in their voice.

The process of character development varies from writer to writer: some find that their characters take on lives of their own during the writing process, and other writers treat their characters like chess pieces and control their every move. It just depends on the sort of writer you are and maybe also on the type of novel you're writing. I find that my characters gradually reveal themselves to me as I embark on each stage of the creation of a novel, and my discoveries about a character will quite often inform the direction of the story.

I created the following character questionnaire as a way to help you kickstart your basic knowledge about your protagonist:

- Who's your main character?
- What's their name?
  (You can change this later, but choosing a name is important—it helps bring your character to life.)
- What's their gender?
- How old are they?
- What do they look like?
  (It might help to imagine somebody you know.)

1. What colour is their hair?
2. Do they have any defining facial features?
3. What's their body shape?
4. What style of clothing do they favour?

- What are their main personality traits?
  (If personality is of particular interest to you, it might pay to research personality types.)
- What's important to your character?
  (Family/mother/father/children? Relationships? Money? Fame? Their fishing boat? Their reputation? Their marble collection? Their career? Their hair? Their eyebrows?)
- What specific actions will define your main character in your novel?
  (It's helpful for your readers to like something about your main character. You'll be creating a balance-of-character scene for this information, so look for a redeeming act: your main character may be a parking officer, but they overlook the illegal parking of people they know to be over 80 years of age; or they might be an unreliable alcoholic, but for every bender they go on, they leave a bottle of champagne for newlyweds at a local resort. If your main character has a redeeming trait, whatever acts come later in

the novel, your readers will know they're fundamentally a good person.)

The character questionnaire provides useful information to call on when you come to outlining your story: it can help you figure out what your main character will lose or gain, and make clear to you their weaknesses, which will be important in terms of the challenges they'll face and how they'll deal with those challenges.

4

Creating An Outline

Up until now, you've been sketching out the basic criteria needed to get started on your outline. An outline may feel rigid to you at first, but don't feel thwarted by the constraints you'll make for yourself here; once you begin to write from your outline, you'll also need to be prepared to meander both within and outside the lines you've drawn for yourself.

While creating your outline, you may feel at times as though you're giving your character a constant battering, but remember, these outline points are just that—points—and you'll come back to it later to buffer those points with extra scenes.

The outline template in chapter *Outline Template* is on its own page, so you can make notes on it or print it easily. Alternatively, use a notebook or Word document to create your own version of the template.

The outline is divided into quarters. To help you understand the function of these, I've labelled them as **intro, reactive, proactive** and **finale**. Each quarter has five points, and every point represents a scene or chapter. That means your whole novel will comprise 20 points of action. This is a similar tool to those often used to create movie scripts. I find it's a useful format from which to springboard the creation of your novel.

Use the following information to fill in your 20 points in your outline template. If you develop more than one event or idea for each point, create a sub-point for each one of these (1a, 1b, 1c, etc.).

Take your time to think each point through, and don't be concerned about getting it perfect the first time you work through it. As you move through each point, refer to your previous points and tweak them if need be. If you become stuck, take a break. You might like to do one of those many activities that have a reputation for freeing up the mind: engage in a different creative task, such as painting, sewing or gardening; or try a more physical activity, such as going for a walk, having a shower, doing some cleaning, going for a drive, watching a movie, reading your favourite book or grabbing a cup of your favourite beverage in your favourite cup—whatever works for you! It's about relaxing the constricting grip on your mind that occurs when you expect too much of it—and then coming back to your outline.

Quarter 1: Intro

Your **first quarter** (Points 1–5) is all about setting up your novel. Here, you'll **introduce** your reader to your characters and their environment. Within this quarter, include your balance-of-character scene where your readers need to witness them behaving in an undeniably 'good' manner. You'll also establish the novel's tone and style; for example, comedic, literary, romantic or fast-paced action. And, importantly, you'll give your reader the event that kicks off your story.

Point 1. Very early in your story, you'll need some intrigue, and this is usually referred to as the **hook**. Your **hook** is the key point that will draw your reader in and have them wanting to read on and find out more. In a murder mystery, this might be a murder. In a romance, it might be characters meeting, possibly hating each other or breaking up.

In literary fiction, it's usually quieter: an odd turn of phrase spoken by a character, an unusual request, an intriguing character, a letter being written or read, or a philosophical dilemma is introduced. In an action novel, it may be an explosion, a collision or a fall from the sky. In drama, it could be an argument or a break-up.

Your **hook** can be as subtle as a few words—'I hate you' or 'I miss my mother'—or as big as a planet exploding.

Think about some **hooks** from your favourite movies or books. What is it about them that makes you ask, 'What happens next?' If you have trouble coming up with a **hook**, use your **What if ... and ... but ...** scenario for now—you can always change it later.

Your **hook** doesn't necessarily need to involve your main character, but it must *concern* your main character and *relate* to them in an important way. The **hook** is a promise to your reader that things are about to get interesting.

Occasionally, an author/editor will take a scene or two from later in the story and add them to the beginning as well to create the **hook**, thus revealing a key scene from the ending, which leaves the reader wondering about the events that have led to that point. For example, at the start of Elizabeth Jolley's *The Well*,[1] there's a flash forward to the scenes that the entire novel revolves around; these scenes then appear again, halfway through the novel, in the correct chronological place.

*Summary: What's your novel's **hook**?*

Point 2. Introduce more detail about your main character. The reader needs to know who this story is about. Who's your central character? What are they doing? What or whom do they love? What's interesting about them? What's happening in their life that's about to change?

What's important to them? What are their hopes and dreams? These are all clues to their journey in your novel, and you can use your character questionnaire to help you here.

Consider your secondary characters and when you might introduce them. It's not necessary to involve them this early on, but somewhere in the **first quarter** is ideal. Who else is in your main character's life who's also important to the story? Now's a good time to introduce your balance-of-character scene where your character shows their good side.

Summary: Who's your story about?

Point 3. Show what's at stake for your character: their relationship, health, car, career, wealth, etc. Here, you're laying the groundwork in preparation for turning your main character's life upside down at Point 5. By showing the reader what's important to your character to maintain, enjoy or create, or the thing your character will protect at all costs, you're also creating a sense of foreboding. Readers understand that, if you're showing it to them, it's important to the story.

Think about what you're going to take away from your main character as you approach Point 5. These two points are directly related: in Point 3, your character's working toward meeting a goal or is enjoying a particular state of mind or way of being. Do they have all the money they need or the desired relationship? Are they on their way to living happily on the Moon? In Point 5, something's going to happen to change this.

Summary: What's at stake for your character?

Point 4. Now it's time to inject your story with a hint of turmoil. Show your reader how what your character loves, what means the most to them or what they're striving for (Point 3) could easily be sabotaged. What might stand in their way? (Dropping a hint is enough here, as you don't want to give the game away.) For example, a love interest might not be the person they seemed, a deer or kangaroo might be hanging around threatening to eat all the food, an accomplice could show signs of becoming an unreliable alcoholic, or a child might pay a lot of attention to a gun. Is your main character grappling with relationship difficulties? Money troubles? Health issues? Think of this point as *poking the bear*. You're giving the reader a clue about what's coming.

Summary: What might stand between your character and what they either want or already have?

Point 5. And ... now's where you make a change to your character's life that throws it into chaos. Pull the rug out from underneath them. Take away / damage / change what they love, need, want or desire. Go on! Do it! You have the power!

Summary: What changes everything for your character?

Quarter 2: Reactive

Your **second quarter** (Points 6–10) is all about your character being **reactive** to the big change in their life that you unleashed in Point 5. In response to what you've just done to this character (don't feel bad!), your story will take a right-hand turn. Your main character is bumbling, fumbling, fleeing and slightly stunned.

Point 6. How does your character react to what you've just done to them? Where do they go? Who do they speak to? Do they disappear into misery? Do they instantly begin scrambling and fighting? Whatever they do, your story has now properly begun, but it's a long way from ending. Your character is now **reactive**, but they're not actually achieving very much yet—and that's okay.

Summary: How does your character react to what's going on?

Point 7. Have your character retreat and reassess their situation. They're having trouble figuring this out. They hit walls, they come up short, they misjudge people, and they second-guess themselves or somebody else in their life. This isn't how they'd planned things would go. They attempt to adapt, but they don't know how to.

Summary: How's your character attempting to adapt to their new reality?

Point 8. Your reader needs to understand clearly *why* your character is struggling. You could try a few devices here, and you can use more than one (but make sure you don't overexplain things, as you don't want your reader to get bored or feel as though you're repeating information). For example, create a backstory scene about your character to explain their difficulty in moving forward (what's happened to them in the past to make them the person they are today?); have a secondary character complain about your main character and point out their failures; include a flashback scene showing that your character is prone to giving up when things become difficult or that they have a hard time adjusting to change; or show the reader something your character doesn't know yet—something that's holding them back.

Summary: Why's your character struggling right now?

Point 9. Show your character making progress in their steps to remedy their situation or achieve their goals, be that in their endeavour to save the universe or create a veggie patch. Have things appear promising: somebody said, 'I love you!'; the car is being repaired; the plants have finally arrived; the spaceship arrives safely; people are listening to your character; speech therapy is going well; or the money comes through. Whatever happens, achievements are made.

Summary: What progress does your character make?

Point 10. Add a shift in the story that will change things as you head into your **third quarter**. This shift should be a surprise to your reader and, especially, to your main character. It could be an unexpected death, a bug in the crop, a fake diamond, the map was upside down, a fatal misjudgement or somebody was wrong about something all along. Here, at Point 10, throw a spanner in the works: something that compromises or endangers the progress made at Point 9.

Summary: Here's a curveball; what is it?

Quarter 3: Proactive

In your **third quarter** (Points 11–15), your character is **proactive**. There's no more feeling lost and not achieving; they don't want their story to end here. They're going to make progress.

Point 11. Things changed for your character in Point 10, and they need to respond to that. Think about how they might do this, in the context of your story, to solve their problem or reach their goals. Does your character need to move location? Enlist help? Repair or obtain an object? Renew a friendship? Obtain repair parts for a vehicle or spacecraft? Change their diet? How do they feel about the course of action they choose? More importantly, what choices do they make?

Summary: What choices will your character make now to get things moving in a positive way?

Point 12. Create a scenario in which your character is confronted emotionally by the recent change in the story. Do they have some inner demons you alluded to in the **first quarter** that they must now face? Do they address a failing that they've previously refused to acknowledge? Is something holding them back? Is their negative talk too persuasive? Are their instincts off-kilter? Is trust an issue for them?

Summary: What is standing in your character's way?

Point 13. But ... something from left field occurs suddenly. Make this one a shocker that your character didn't see coming. Many stories or movies will have a momentous event happen around this three-quarter point. All hell breaks loose. This may be a physically huge event, some words spoken by another character, perhaps an unsent email, a tweet that goes viral or a thought that should have been verbalised. Everything turns on a pinhead right now, and it all relates to your character's needs, desires, dreams, hopes and goals. To help you close in on this event, think of words such as 'intimidation', 'danger' and 'implications'. Imagine your character opening an unknown door; what do they see?

Summary: What's the momentous event in which all hell breaks loose?

Point 14. A lot has happened, so now we need to give your reader a breather and bring the pace down a notch. Think of the quieter moments in a song before the final crescendo—that's what this is. Think about introspection, contemplation, self-care, organising, building things up or tearing things down, physically or emotionally.

Summary: What's the calm before the final storm?

Point 15. Have your character learn or discover something new that can kickstart their home run in the final quarter. Did they find the key (literally or figuratively) to new information? Is there new evidence to support an idea? Do they reconnect with a secondary character from earlier in your novel? (Remember, no new characters should appear now; if you find you do need a new character, find a place for them in your **first quarter**). Did the last point give your character some insight, strength, hope or understanding to use in this final stretch?

Summary: Give your character something to help them achieve their goal or solve their problem.

Quarter 4: Finale

The **fourth quarter** (Points 16–20) is when you bring the story home and close your narrative arc.

Point 16. Your character gained new insight in Point 15. They now have new knowledge, views or opinions, and they're on the final leg of their journey. Now's when they make decisions or take actions that are positive and useful as they move toward resolving their problems or achieving their goals.

Summary: What actions or steps does your character now take to get them one step closer to achieving their goal or solving their problem?

Point 17. Leave a clue in your story about information your character missed earlier in their story—information they need now that's been there all along. Is there a person in their life they should have spoken to before, and they finally speak to this person now? Did their personality or a person, place or thing get in the way of them learning or understanding something? As the writer, this may have you looking back over your previous points to make some adjustments.

Summary: What did your character fail to see or do earlier in the novel that they see or do now?

Point 18. Now's when your main character needs to show some inner strength. Your reader's attention is on them to bring the story to its resolution. Your character needs to be confident. They may have any number of failings—being clumsy, obnoxious, self-conscious or vain—but now's when they need to have faith in their own actions and a clear idea of their goals. Show your character making the right choices, but in the context of their capabilities and personality.

Summary: What action does your character decide to take to resolve the story?

Point 19. This is when your main character finally gets what they want: they achieve their goal or solve their problem with a resounding show of strength, intelligence and resilience. Whatever they achieve here, the reader should be cheering them on.

Summary: How does your character achieve their goal or solve their problem?

Point 20. The story is almost over. Tie up any loose ends or unanswered questions. This is the time for denouements. You may even introduce a minor twist to remind the reader that your character's story will continue beyond what they've just lived through, or to hint at a planned series. Perhaps you might leave a taste of what's to come in your next novel, but for this story, don't leave your reader hanging—give them the satisfaction of an ending. You can choose to go out with a bang (a birth, a marriage, an accident, a death, or a literal or figurative slamming of a door) or more calmly (driving or sailing away, swinging on a swing, finishing a marathon, gazing out the window, or singing a song). Perhaps you could tie it in with, or repeat in a different way, an action from your very first chapter.

Summary: How will you wrap up your novel?

[1] Jolley, E. (1986). *The Well.* Viking Press, Docklands, Australia.

5

Outline Template A

Intro
1

2

3

4

5

Reactive
6

7

8

9

10

6

Outline Template B

Proactive
11

12

13

14

15

Finale
16

17

18

19

20

7

Filling In Your Outline

Now you've created a solid outline, you're almost ready to start writing. Don't worry if you've left points out or if there are some points you feel aren't strong—you can fill these in or rework them as your story develops. The outline is an incredibly useful guide, but it's also very pliable, and you can move points around or change them as you write and start to get a clearer sense of your novel's overall shape and trajectory.

The next step is to start turning your points—the skeleton of your story—into scenes. As you do this, you might realise you need additional scenes that you haven't included in your initial outline; for example, scenes that move your characters from place to place (either physically or emotionally). You may also notice other narrative elements that you'll need to work on, such as pace, rhythm and a narrative arc, but for now, focus on the key scenes you've created that move your character through those four quarters of **intro, reactive, proactive** and **finale**. Keep in mind our original dictum: you can't edit a blank page. Our focus is still on getting your first draft written.

Start at Point 1. Put whatever you wrote for Point 1 in your outline at the top of your first manuscript page, and then begin writing this point as a scene. I suggest you keep your story simple—at least to begin with—and don't get bogged down in its potential twists and turns.

Write what you want to write, rather than what you feel you should write. You're not aiming for perfection, and don't think about spelling or punctuation.

Here are some useful tools you can use as you embark on the writing process:

Funnelling. To catch the words that wait to be written, I like to imagine a funnelling tool. You now have the information you need to get started on filling in your outline, and so many words and tangents wait in your mind to spill onto the page. In this moment, your outline helps you to stay on track and keep focussed, and you should allow those words to pour down the funnel freely and into your outline, in a stream-of-consciousness flow.

Word prompts. Word prompts are excellent for drawing out useful scenarios and memories from deep in your mind. You'll be amazed at what you can find in that grey matter of yours! I supply word prompts on my Instagram account, @writerjulieproudfoot, or you can randomly choose your own words from books, magazines, etc. Find two words, and with your outline in mind, commit to including them in that day's writing. Try starting a sentence with one, and then see where it takes you.

Three pages. I find that making a commitment to fill three pages when I sit down to write is a useful target. Three pages is approximately 1,000 words, which is a very achievable length; it's a good size for a scene or chapter, and you can shorten or lengthen it as needed. Depending on your circumstances, you'll discover what suits you best—this might be 500 words a day or 3,000 words per week—but creating a routine to stick to will help you achieve results. Sit yourself down, write your outline at the top of the page, choose your word prompts and any other tools you plan to use, and go. Don't stop until the words you've committed to are written, no matter the quality or content.

I first began writing three pages daily while working through Julia Cameron's *The Artist's Way*,[1] which requires you to write three pages of your diary every day. Producing that amount of writing in one session has become muscle memory and is now automatic for me.

Senses. As with word prompts, choosing to add one sense per chapter is a great way to include visceral content/detail that a reader can relate to, and that lends texture and interest to your writing. Remember to have your characters smell, taste, touch and hear, and always have them see.

Three people. Include at least three people in every scene. They don't need to be physically present, but having three people either active, thought of or discussed in each chapter is an effective tool for maintaining intrigue and momentum.

The unknown. A fun tool to use is to have the reader and/or secondary characters know something about your main character that they do not themselves know. It creates tension and intrigue for the reader, and you can control if and when this information is revealed.

Dialogue. Good dialogue is key for keeping a reader engaged while moving your story along. Dialogue is fun and full of energy, and it's a great way for your reader to visualise characters and to get information across, but getting it right can require a lengthy process of editing. Properly edited written dialogue isn't the same as the conversation that you have with friends and family. Real conversation is filled with pauses, ums, repetition and explanations that are unnecessary when trying to get information across. A character's individuality needs to be clear for the reader to understand who said what. This can be helped by throwing in an occasional name ('You're missing a shoe, Ben!') and by keeping in mind the character's own personality: are they a gentle person who speaks with common words and uses soft consonants (e.g. f, h or w), or are they full of life and use punchy, short words with heavy consonants (e.g. g, c or b)?

I suggest getting the dialogue written, without restraint, then going back through it to pare it back by cutting words that aren't essential to getting the information across. Trust your judgement and know that you can come back and add words back in later.

Avoid long passages of description with no dialogue, and also avoid long passages of dialogue with no descriptions; both of these can become dreary for a reader. You can buffer dialogue with descriptions of your characters' movements, their surroundings, other characters' appearance or actions, food, weather, etc.

Character chats. If you're struggling for words and direction, a great tool to use to get things moving again is to throw two or more of your characters together for a chat. Choose a place—a car, an elevator or a café—and have them talk it out. Use dialogue only; remember, this is just an exercise to help you get unstuck. You could start them off with something like this: 'Hey, I saw you the other day, but you didn't see me.'

You might find that you discover new things about your characters to use in your story or you might use the conversation, or part of it, in a scene. Dialogue is alive with movement and opinion: people dodge each other, hide things or try to exert influence. Enjoy finding your characters' true personalities with this tool.

By working within your framework, you'll free yourself up to focus on your story and achieve real forward momentum with your writing. You'll give yourself the best chance of capturing your words into your funnel and pouring them onto the page.

[1] Cameron, J. (2020). *The Artist's Way*. Souvenir Press, London, UK.

8

Moving Forward

Congratulations! You now have your first draft up your sleeve, and you're ready to move on to the next step! This is a great achievement, and it's time for celebration. I hope it's been an invigorating and productive process for you.

Now that you have the bones of your story down, you might be keen to develop your draft into a polished manuscript. I'd suggest that the next move for you will be to skim through your work from start to finish and tidy up your sentences and punctuation to have your novel in a readable state. You're not aiming for perfection here, but you are preparing your work for you to read through it unimpeded by typographical errors, poor punctuation, or incorrect grammar, all of which make it difficult to read; you want a piece of work that doesn't cause you to wonder what on earth you meant when you wrote it down.

With minor errors now cleared up, your manuscript is ready for you to assess. You'll want to look at the overall work you've created and make decisions on structural improvements. I do this with a printed hard copy of my manuscript, but you might prefer to do this on a screen.

As you read, make regular notes about what's not working: where you'd like to add scenes that will move characters from place to place, fill in gaps in information or add new points of action; where you can weave in deeper thought and introspection; where you might add the finer detail of objects, faces or places; or where you'd like to increase the pace or calm the energy down (again, think of music slowing or speeding up, soft or loud). Ultimately, you're making plans to fill out your novel and nourish it with the substance to create a more enjoyable and engaging read.

Your first draft may be mostly action and movement, where you've funnelled all those words from your thoughts into your outline, and you've created a specific story and characters; now, you'll embellish what you've created and give your work heart.

9

Final Tips And Tricks

Tense. Which tense are you writing in? **Past tense?** (e.g. 'Anne walked' / 'Anne saw' / 'Anne loved') **Present tense?** (e.g. 'Anne walks' / 'Anne sees' / 'Anne loves').

Tense is more complex than this, and you might wish to research it some more. For ease of reading and understanding, stick to your chosen tense within each chapter; if you really need to switch tense, place a break to define your switch.

Point of view (POV). When you sit down to write, decide which kind of narrator you're going to be. A writer's choice is often dictated by the kind of story being written, and it positions the writer in one of four places: *first person*, *second person*, *third person* (*limited* or *omniscient*) or *dramatic*.

First-person POV. This POV uses the pronouns I, we, me, etc. (e.g. 'I am' / 'I do' / 'I will' / 'I was'). Writing in the first person is often considered the easiest POV. It places you, as the writer, immediately in the character's mind. The first-person POV is used when writing an autobiography or memoir, but it can also be used when writing fiction.

To write in the first person, it helps to imagine that you are the character whose POV you're writing from.

Second-person POV. This POV isn't often used in fiction. It's the POV used in letter writing. Think of it as one character speaking to another character. (e.g. 'you are' / 'you did' / 'you will' / 'you were'). If you include a letter in your novel, it might be written in second-person POV.

Third-person limited POV. This is the most commonly used narration POV. It uses the character's name or pronouns he/she/they (e.g. 'Rachel is' / 'Rachel does' / 'Rachel will' / 'Rachel was'). The narrator stays with one character's POV at a time. To help you do this, visualise the scenes through your character's eyes. You shouldn't describe things the POV character cannot see; for example, your character cannot see around corners or know what another character is thinking, and they can't see their own face. Don't make descriptions of your character by having them look in a mirror—it'll be immediately clear to your reader that this is what you're doing, and it will bring the reader out of the story and have them thinking about you as the writer rather than your characters. Using the mirror might appear contrived or have your reader believing your character to be self-obsessed, all for the sake of showing the reader information that's most likely unnecessary.

Third-person omniscient POV. This narrator knows how all characters in your story feel and think and what they all see at any given time. As this narrator, you have an all-access backstage pass to all characters' knowledge. As with the third-person limited POV, you're using characters' names or he/she/they pronouns, but you have access to all characters' knowledge.

Dramatic POV or fly-on-the-wall POV. This POV is often used in screenplay writing and rarely used in fiction writing, but it can be a useful exercise to try on for a scene or two. The-fly-on-the-wall viewpoint doesn't give access to a character's thoughts, feelings or emotions, as 'fly-on-the-wall' suggests. This POV can only see movement, sound or objects, and only those of the characters visible to the 'fly'. Try writing a scene using this POV; it'll highlight the physicality of a scene.

As with tense, *stick to one POV within a chapter*; if you do switch POV, make it clear by using a section break.

Head-hopping. If you switch between characters' POVs, try to restrict this to one character per chapter, and make it clear from the beginning of the chapter whose head it is you're in: you might name each chapter after the character whose voice it's in, or have each character speak or think about another character or about their environment to help your reader understand which character they're inhabiting, and give each character a voice that's distinctive from other characters. Don't give your reader whiplash by switching mid-chapter.

Have a point. Ensure that each paragraph has a point or reason for being where it is, and that it moves logically to the next paragraph in terms of time, space and/or thought. It may be that a paragraph is purely for moving a character from one place to another.

Read out loud. One of your most valuable tools as a writer is reading your work out loud—mistakes and lack of rhythm will become very clear. To take it a step further, you can record yourself reading; this isn't necessarily to listen to the recording afterward—although you can do this, and it's also useful—but the act of pronouncing words with an audience in mind makes it clear to you how the words might sound in a reader's mind, and it points out to you words that are clumsy to read or pronounce, or sentences that are awkward and stumble over themselves.

If you take your novel through to publishing and find yourself reading your novel to an audience in a bookshop or at a festival, you'll be thankful that you practised recording yourself reading. I stumbled on this strategy while recording a story for an audio-story website, and I've kept it in my toolbox of tips and tricks ever since.

Themes. This is a tricky one. Elizabeth Jolley once said that if you don't know what your themes are, your readers will tell you; by this, she means you should be aware of your themes. If you aren't, it may come as a shock when a reader figures it out before you do. It's easy for readers to tell you what your themes are because they have a degree of emotional distance from the story that you, as the writer, don't have.

If you ask a reader what a book is about, they'll often tell you the theme: it's about unrequited love, it's a rags-to-riches story or it's a coming-of-age story. Your theme is what your story is actually about. It's the message underlying the story—its key takeaway. Confusingly, this can be subjective; one reader's takeaway may differ from another's.

Themes aren't the same as plot. Plot is what happens; for example, Bill becomes a gambler, Bill loses everything, Bill's wife leaves him, Bill becomes homeless, and then Bill recovers and becomes a gambling counsellor. Themes represent the *meaning* behind the story; in Bill's story, the theme is fall from grace or redemption.

You may be thinking, *Hey, I don't have a message; I just like to write stories.* That's fine too, but you'll probably find themes develop naturally and make themselves known once your story is written. Themes are the backbone of a story. The stronger your story becomes as you edit, the more your themes will become apparent.

Once you understand your theme, the writing work becomes a tiny bit easier too. But if you enjoy a more meandering style of writing, figuring out your theme is more difficult. If you find it hard to pinpoint your theme, leave it alone until you've moved through a few more drafts.

Reading. The greatest source of all for learning to write is reading. Read great books to get a feel for what you love and how it's done. Even not-so-great books can help you understand what it is about a story that doesn't work, and how or why it doesn't work. Read to learn about storytelling, sentence structure, rhythm and pace, and always read to know the simple pleasure of reading.

Sharing your work. Every writer works differently, but before I share my writing, I've worked through at least 10 drafts. Two for structure, two for chapter detail, two for paragraph detail, two for sentences, two for punctation and grammar, and this is all after I have completed a few drafts that were simply writing the story.

Over time, you'll come to know who of your readers understands the writing you're trying to achieve, and who it is that you're most comfortable working with. Be patient with yourself and your reader, as you'll have different perspectives on the work, and that's ultimately how you'll move forward.

When you share your work, make it clear to your reader what you require of them. If you're looking for constructive feedback, ask them what it is you'd like to know. Is it only structure that you'd like feedback on? Perhaps it's only whether the story makes sense? Is it punctuation you need advice on? And remember that, unless you ask them to tell you what works well in your story, your reader will believe it to be more useful to tell you what's not working in your writing. You've worked hard to achieve your manuscript, so you may find it difficult at first (and be surprised that you didn't see it yourself) to hear what's not working.

If you'd like to send your work to an agent or publisher, I suggest you employ an editor first to give you professional feedback. An editor offers a range of services from manuscript appraisal to line editing, and it'll increase your chances of having a publisher pay attention to your work.

A note on health. Often when people sit down to embark on a lengthy period of writing, they don't think about their health. And why should they? They're focussed on writing! But there are a few things you might like to keep in mind. If you're not already on board with the standing-desk revolution, it might be something to consider investing in. Writers often develop issues with backs and knees, but sitting still and staring at a screen for hours at a time can also affect your other organs: heart, thyroid, eyes, liver and lungs—all the things that become stagnant during prolonged sitting. Think about taking regular standing-up breaks and/or incorporating exercise—such as walking, stretching, yoga or swimming—into your routine.

Julie Proudfoot is an author of fiction, poetry and non-fiction. Her first published novel, The Neighbour, won the Seizure Viva La Novella Prize. She holds bachelor's degrees in psychology, anthropology, and sociology. Julie has appeared at Bendigo Writers Festival, Queenscliffe Literary Festival, Perth Writers Festival, and The Melbourne Emerging Writer's Festival. She draws on her degrees in Psychology, Anthropology and Philosophy to inform her work. Julie writes from her home in Queensland, Australia.

Thank you to editors
Melissa-Jane Nguyen, Carody Culver, and Lindsay Corten
for their contributions to *Kickstart Your Novel*.
Without their fresh and professional input, this book wouldn't have been possible.
Their work here has been invaluable.

Let it go. Let it out.
Let it all unravel.
Let it free and it can be.
A path on which to travel.
— Michael Leunig[1]

---

[1] Leunig, M. (n.d.). *Let it go.* https://www.leunig.com.au/works/poems

www.ingramcontent.com/pod-product-compliance
Lightning Source LLC
Chambersburg PA
CBHW020431010526
44118CB00010B/533